D0570971

EDUCATION & TRAINING

Exploring Career Pathways

Diane Lindsey Reeves

Created and produced by
Bright Futures Press, Cary, North Carolina
www.brightfuturespress.com

Published by
Cherry Lake Publishing, Ann Arbor, Michigan
www.cherrylakepublishing.com

Photo Credits: Cover, BeautyLine; page 7, legenda, Robert Kneschke, Monkey Business Images, Den Rise, iofoto, Tyler Olson, Monkey Business Images, Monkey Business Images; page 8, legenda; page 10, Robert Kneschke; page 12, Monkey Business Images; page 14, Den Rise; page 16, ilfoto; page 18, Tyler Olson; page 20, Money Business Images; page 22, Monkey Business Images; page 24, Oleg Krugliak.

Library of Congress Cataloging-in-Publication Date

CIP data has been filed and is available at catalog.loc.gov.

Printed in the United States of America.

TABLE OF CONTENTS

Hello, World of Work...4

Take a Hike..6

WoW Up Close...7

    Animal Trainer..8

    Child Care Director...10

    Coach..12

    Distance Learning Coordinator...............................14

    Elementary Teacher..16

    Media Specialist...18

    Principal...20

    School Counselor..22

WoW Big List...24

Take Your Pick..26

Explore Some More...27

My WoW..30

Glossary...31

Index...32

HELLO WORLD OF WORK

This is you.

Right now, your job is to go to school and learn all you can.

This is the world of work.

It's where people earn a living, find purpose in their lives, and make the world a better place.

Sooner or later, you'll have to find your way from

HERE to THERE.

To get started, take all the jobs in the incredibly enormous world of work and organize them into an imaginary pile. It's a big pile, isn't it? It would be pretty tricky to find the perfect job for you among so many options.

No worries!

Some very smart career experts have made it easier to figure out. They sorted jobs and industries into groups by the types of skills and products they share. These groups are called career clusters. They provide pathways that will make it easier for you to find career options that match your interests.

Architecture & Construction

Arts & Communication

Business & Administration

Education & Training

Finance

Food & Natural Resources

Government

Health Sciences

Hospitality & Tourism

Human Services

Information Technology

Law & Public Safety

Manufacturing

Marketing, Sales & Service

Science, Technology, Engineering & Mathematics (STEM)

Transportation

Good thing you are still a kid.

You have lots of time to explore ideas and imagine yourself doing all kinds of amazing things. The **World of Work** (WoW for short) series of books will help you get started.

TAKE A HIKE!

There are 16 career pathways waiting for you to explore. The only question is: Which one should you explore first?

Is **Education and Training** a good path for you to start exploring career ideas? There is a lot to like about this pathway. These professionals teach all kinds of people—from babies to senior citizens and everyone in between. They help people with problems find jobs and get the skills they need to succeed. The work they do changes lives and makes the world a better place.

See if any of the following questions grab your interest.

WOULD YOU ENJOY babysitting, teaching your grandparents how to use a computer, or running a summer camp for neighbor kids in your backyard?

CAN YOU IMAGINE someday working at a college counseling center, corporate training center, or school?

ARE YOU CURIOUS ABOUT what animal trainers, coaches, college professors, guidance counselors, or principals do?

If so, it's time to take a hike! Keep reading to see what kinds of opportunities you can discover along the Education and Training pathway.

But wait!

What if you don't think you'll like this pathway?

You have two choices.

You could keep reading, to find out more than you already know. You might be surprised to learn how many amazing careers you'll find along this path.

OR

Turn to page 27 to get ideas about other WoW pathways.

SCHOOL COUNSELOR

ANIMAL TRAINER

PRINCIPAL

MEDIA SPECIALIST

WoW Up Close

They teach children to read. They teach employees how to use new technologies. They help people with problems. They run child care centers, schools, and colleges. These are just some of the important jobs that people who work along the Education and Training pathway do.

COACH

ELEMENTARY TEACHER

ONLINE LEARNING

CHILD CARE DIRECTOR

DISTANCE LEARNING COORDINATOR

ANIMAL TRAINER

Let's say you have a dog as a pet. You have taught him the usual tricks. He can sit, stay, and speak at your command (or with the bribe of a treat). Did you know that many dogs are capable of so much more?

With special training, they can learn how to be **therapy dogs**, service animals, or performers. Some dogs even work with the police or the military and sniff out drugs or bombs or search for lost people.

Animal trainers are the people to thank for making good things like these happen with animals. Whether training pets to act "civilized" or teaching dolphins to jump through hoops, animal trainers are first and foremost animal lovers. They have great respect for the creatures they work with and do all they can to take good care of them.

It is pretty amazing to see a well-trained animal in action. For instance, a service dog can be trained to be the "eyes" of a blind person, helping them navigate streets and stairs. They can also be trained to be the "ears" of a hearing-impaired person, alerting them to ringing telephones or doorbells.

Some hospitals and elder care centers use animals to provide therapy for human patients. The comfort of spending time with a well-trained animal can help people recover from injuries and cope with health problems. It's another way of proving that a good dog can be man's best friend!

Check It Out!

Go online to explore the animal kingdom at

- http://www.animalplanet.com
- http://channel.nationalgeographic.com/wild
- http://www.thezooonline.com

Start Now!

- ✔ If you have a pet, try teaching it some new tricks.
- ✔ Go online to research your favorite species of animals.
- ✔ Start a pet-sitting business to help friends and neighbors when they are away from their pets.

CHILD CARE DIRECTOR

Every day, millions of parents drop their young children off at child care centers before they go to work. They are looking for safe, nurturing care, healthy meals, and a nice mix of fun and learning for their children. It is up to **child care directors** to make sure that parents and their children get what they need.

There are all types of child care centers and all sizes, too. Those based in a person's home may care for a few children under the age of five. Child care centers can hold more than 100 children—from babies to school-age kids who come for **after-school care**.

As you can probably imagine, child care directors have a lot to do. They are in charge of the staff, so they hire and train teachers and caregivers, plan schedules, and handle payroll. They plan menus and order food supplies. They plan lessons and activities for each age group. They also work with the children's parents, keeping them informed about their child's progress and handling any problems.

In bigger child care centers, other people help with some of these tasks, but it is still up to the director to make sure that everything gets done right. Without good child care, other people can't do their jobs, so this kind of work is especially important.

Check It Out!

Go online and compare different child care centers in your community. Simply use a search engine to look up the name of each center. If you were a parent, which one would you want your child to attend?

Start Now!

- Check into taking a babysitting class at your local YMCA (http://www.ymca.net) or Red Cross chapter (http://www.redcross.org).

- Volunteer to read stories to younger children at a nearby child care center or library.

- Make a brochure describing what you think would be an ideal child care center.

COACH

If you have ever played a sport, you have probably worked with a **coach**. Someone took the time (and showed the patience!) to teach you and your teammates how to play a game. Maybe it was a team sport like T-ball, basketball, or soccer. Maybe it was an individual sport like tennis or golf.

Whatever the sport, players need to learn the skills, strategies, and rules of the game. That's what coaches do.

Some coaches are parents who volunteer to help coach their own children's teams. In middle and high schools, coaches often teach other types of classes during the day and then coach the school's sports teams after school. At the college and professional sports level, coaches work full-time to prepare winning teams. Professional coaches are also found in sports clubs.

As nice as winning is, it isn't everything. A big part of being a good coach is motivating players to be the best they can be. As one famous coach named Tom Landry put it, "A coach is someone who tells you what you don't want to hear, and has you see what you don't want to see, so you can be who you have always known you can be."

Check It Out!

Who do you think is the best coach of all time? Vince Lombardi? Yogi Berra? John Wooden? Mike Krzyzewski? Ask your parents for their ideas and use the Internet to find out more about them.

Start Now!

- Watch professional sports games on TV and pay attention to how the coaches interact with the players.
- Volunteer to help coach a team of younger kids at your local community center.
- Pick a favorite sport and make a poster explaining the most important rules and moves.

DISTANCE LEARNING COORDINATORS

Schools aren't the only places where learning happens. More and more people are taking classes online. This includes students young and old. It is even possible to earn a degree from a good college from the comfort of your own home.

Pretty much anything you can do in a classroom you can do online. Teachers give lectures that students can see and hear on their own computers. They lead discussions among students and provide learning materials that students can download and read. Students submit their homework assignments online, and teachers provide comments, answer questions, and deliver grades as needed. Online schools make learning possible anytime and anywhere!

Distance learning coordinators help make this possible by doing what it takes to keep things running smoothly for both students and teachers. This includes making sure that the online "classroom" is easy to use and that teachers and students can keep in touch with each other. Coordinators plan courses and manage the registration process. They make sure that teachers are doing a good job and that the students are receiving quality learning experiences.

Actually, a lot of what distance learning coordinators do is similar to what a principal would do at a regular school. A big word used to describe what they do is **administration**.

Check It Out!

Explore free online classes for kids at

▶ http://www.e-learningforkids.org

Start Now!

- ✔ Make a list of things you'd like to learn more about.

- ✔ Think of something you know how to do well, and use a smartphone or digital camera to record yourself explaining how to do it.

- ✔ Start noticing the types of things your teachers do to make learning more interesting.

ELEMENTARY TEACHER

Given that you've spent a fair share of your time in the classroom with elementary teachers, this is a career you probably know a lot about. But have you ever stopped to think about what the job really involves?

One of the most important (and exciting!) things that elementary teachers do is teach children how to read. If learning were a house, then reading would be the **foundation** that all the other subjects sit on. When a child learns to read, the whole world of learning opens up to them. It really is that important.

Elementary students tend to stay in a classroom with the same teacher for most of the day. So, these teachers also teach many other subjects, including math, language arts, writing, science, and social studies. Other teachers teach the "specials" like art, music, technology, and physical education. But, for the most part, elementary teachers need to know a lot about many subjects in order to do their jobs.

Working with children day in and day out, making lesson plans, grading papers, and planning activities keep teachers very busy. In fact, there are times when the work is very demanding. But most teachers would agree that helping children learn is always rewarding.

Check It Out!

Learn something new at

- http://kids.nationalgeographic.com
- http://mathforum.org/dr.math
- https://kids.usa.gov
- http://www.factmonster.com/homework

Start Now!

- Go online to find resources you can use to make a lesson plan to teach about a topic you are interested in.
- Volunteer to read with a younger student.
- Ask your parent or grandparent to tell you about their favorite elementary teacher.

MEDIA SPECIALIST

Once upon a time, media specialists were called librarians. Libraries were places you visited only when you needed to borrow a book.

Nowadays, media specialists still help you borrow books from the library. But they are just as likely to help you find information on a computer or smartphone! Now technology is almost as big a part of the library as books.

Today's media specialists are an important part of a school. They work with whole classes and individual students to show them how to get information from books, Web sites, magazines, newspapers, and other sources. They teach students how to tell quality information from fake news and how to use that information in their schoolwork.

Media specialists work with teachers to choose books, software, and other educational materials that support the topics being taught in each grade. An important part of their job is to make learning more fun and interesting for students.

Check It Out!

Read and listen to biographies about famous children's book authors like J. K. Rowling, R. L. Stine, and Dr. Seuss at

http://bit.ly/KidsBookBios

Start Now!

- Make list of your 10 favorite children's books.

- Ask your school media specialist to help you find copies of the latest **Newbery** and **Caldecott** award-winners for children's literature.

- Write a story about the imaginary adventures of a school media specialist.

PRINCIPAL

A **principal** is the boss of a school. He or she is in charge of the teachers, the students, and the staff. It is the principal's job to create a place where learning happens.

That means the school is safe, clean, and well-organized. It means that teachers have the skills and resources they need to do their jobs. It means that healthy meals are provided and kids have places to play. The list of their responsibilities goes on and on.

The best principals are good leaders. They lead by their example and try to bring out the best in every student. The good ones know how to have fun with the students. But they also make it clear that they mean business when it comes to students behaving themselves and doing their schoolwork.

Being a principal is a big job, and it takes special skill and training to learn how to do it. Most principals start out as teachers. They have to go back to college and get a special degree in order to qualify for a job leading a school. Good schools are always led by good principals!

Check It Out!

See what a day in the life of a principal is like at

▶ http://bit.ly/PrincipalDay1

▶ http://bit.ly/PrincipalDay2

▶ http://bit.ly/PrincipalDay3

Start Now!

- ✔ Create a list of the changes you would make at your school if you were the principal.

- ✔ Ask your school principal what the favorite part of his or her job is.

- ✔ Get some leadership experience by running for a position on your student council.

SCHOOL COUNSELOR

School counselors work to make sure that students are on track in their studies now and are prepared to do well in the future. They work with students in three different areas: academic success, career exploration and planning, and social and emotional development needs.

Add the fact that most school counselors work with hundreds of students, and you'll see just how big a job school counselors have.

Here are some of the things that a school counselor might do on a typical day. They might put together a career fair for students to explore interesting options for their future. They might talk to students about the types of courses they need to take in high school or make a presentation to students and parents about educational opportunities available after high school. They might talk to a class or a small group of students about bully prevention. School counselors also work with individual students who are struggling with big problems at home or school.

It is easy to see why school counselors are such a valuable part of the educational team. Theirs is a caring profession, and they make a big difference in the lives of the students they serve.

Check It Out!

Explore issues that school counselors care about at

▶ http://www.pacerkidsagainstbullying.org

▶ http://pbskids.org/itsmylife

▶ https://www.mynextmove.org

Start Now!

✔ Make a poster encouraging kids to do their best in school.

✔ Ask a friend what they want to be when they grow up and help them find out more about that career.

✔ Find out if your school has a peer mediation program and get involved.

Academic advisor • Academic affairs dean • Activity director • Adapted physical education teacher • Admissions director • Adult basic education instructor • Aerobics instructor • **ANIMAL TRAINER** • Archivist • Assistant principal • Assistant professor • Associate professor • Athletic director • Audiovisual technician • Author • Career and technical education instructor • Career center director • Career counselor • Career technical supervisor • Chief learning officer • Chief wellness officer • **CHILD CARE DIRECTOR** • Children's librarian • **COACH** • College president • Computer science instructor • Coordinator of online

WoW Big List

Take a look at some of the different kinds of jobs people do in the Education and Training pathway. **WoW!**

Some of these job titles will be familiar to you. Others will be so unfamiliar that you will scratch your head and say "huh?"

programs • Criminal justice instructor • Curriculum and assessment director • Curriculum and instruction director • Curriculum coordinator • Dean of students • Dietician • **DISTANCE LEARNING COORDINATOR** • Early head start director • Education coordinator • **ELEMENTARY TEACHER** • English as a second language (ESL) instructor • Financial aid director • Fitness coordinator • Fitness instructor • Flight instructor

• Foreign language instructor • Forestry and conservation instructor • General education development (GED) teacher • Guidance counselor • Health specialties instructor • High school teacher • Historian • History instructor • Instructional designer • Instruction systems specialist • Law instructor • Library director • Library science instructor • Literacy teacher • Mathematical science instructor • **MEDIA SPECIALIST** • Middle school teacher • Museum curator • Multimedia service coordinator • Nutritionist • Online facilitator • Personal trainer • Physical education teacher • Poet • Preschool director • Preschool teacher • **PRINCIPAL**

Find a job title that makes you curious. Type the name of the job into your favorite Internet search engine and find out more about the people who have that job.

1 What do they do?

2 Where do they work?

3 How much training do they need to do this job?

• Provost • Psychology instructor • Recreation and fitness instructor • Recreation supervisor • Registrar • Regulatory affairs consultant • Religion instructor • School administrator • Science instructor • **SCHOOL COUNSELOR** • School standards coach • School superintendent • Scout • Site director • Sociology instructor • Special education director • Teacher's assistant • Translator • Tutor • Writer • Yoga instructor

TAKE YOUR PICK

	Put stars next to your 3 favorite career ideas	Put an X next to the career idea you like the least	Put a question mark next to the career idea you want to learn more about
Animal trainer			
Child care director			
Coach			
Distance learning coordinator			
Elementary teacher			
Media specialist			
Principal			
School counselor			
	What do you like most about these careers?	What is it about this career that doesn't appeal to you?	What do you want to learn about this career? Where can you find answers?

Which Big Wow List ideas are you curious about?

EXPLORE SOME MORE

The Education and Training pathway is only one of 16 career pathways that hold exciting options for your future. Take a look at the other 15 to figure out where to start exploring next.

Architecture & Construction

WOULD YOU ENJOY making things with LEGOs™, building a treehouse or birdhouse, or designing the world's best skate park?

CAN YOU IMAGINE someday working at a construction site, a design firm, or a building company?

ARE YOU CURIOUS ABOUT what civil engineers, demolition technicians, heavy-equipment operators, landscape architects, or urban planners do?

Arts & Communication

WOULD YOU ENJOY drawing your own cartoons, using your smartphone to make a movie, or writing articles for the student newspaper?

CAN YOU IMAGINE someday working at a Hollywood movie studio, a publishing company, or a television news station?

ARE YOU CURIOUS ABOUT what actors, bloggers, graphic designers, museum curators, or writers do?

Business & Administration

WOULD YOU ENJOY playing Monopoly, being the boss of your favorite club or team, or starting your own business?

CAN YOU IMAGINE someday working at a big corporate headquarters, government agency, or international business center?

ARE YOU CURIOUS ABOUT what brand managers, chief executive officers, e-commerce analysts, entrepreneurs, or purchasing agents do?

Finance

WOULD YOU ENJOY earning and saving money, being the class treasurer, or playing the stock market game?

CAN YOU IMAGINE someday working at an accounting firm, bank, or Wall Street stock exchange?

ARE YOU CURIOUS ABOUT what accountants, bankers, fraud investigators, property managers, or stockbrokers do?

Food & Natural Resources

WOULD YOU ENJOY exploring nature, growing your own garden, or setting up a recycling center at your school?

CAN YOU IMAGINE someday working at a national park, raising crops in a city farm, or studying food in a laboratory?

ARE YOU CURIOUS ABOUT what landscape architects, chefs, food scientists, environmental engineers, or forest rangers do?

 ## Government

WOULD YOU ENJOY reading about U.S. presidents, running for student council, or helping a favorite candidate win an election?

CAN YOU IMAGINE someday working at a chamber of commerce, government agency, or law firm?

ARE YOU CURIOUS about what mayors, customs agents, federal special agents, intelligence analysts, or politicians do?

Health Sciences

WOULD YOU ENJOY nursing a sick pet back to health, dissecting animals in a science lab, or helping the school coach run a sports clinic?

CAN YOU IMAGINE someday working at a dental office, hospital, or veterinary clinic?

ARE YOU CURIOUS ABOUT what art therapists, doctors, dentists, pharmacists, and veterinarians do?

 ## Hospitality & Tourism

WOULD YOU ENJOY traveling, sightseeing, or meeting people from other countries?

CAN YOU IMAGINE someday working at a convention center, resort, or travel agency?

ARE YOU CURIOUS ABOUT what convention planners, golf pros, tour guides, resort managers, or wedding planners do?

 ## Human Services

WOULD YOU ENJOY showing a new kid around your school, organizing a neighborhood food drive, or being a peer mediator?

CAN YOU IMAGINE someday working at an elder care center, fitness center, or mental health center?

ARE YOU CURIOUS ABOUT what elder care center directors, hairstylists, personal trainers, psychologists, or religious leaders do?

Information Technology

WOULD YOU ENJOY creating your own video game, setting up a Web site, or building your own computer?

CAN YOU IMAGINE someday working at an information technology start-up company, software design firm, or research and development laboratory?

ARE YOU CURIOUS ABOUT what artificial intelligence scientists, big data analysts, computer forensic investigators, software engineers, or video game designers do?

Law & Public Safety

WOULD YOU ENJOY working on the school safety patrol, participating in a mock court trial at school, or coming up with a fire escape plan for your home?

CAN YOU IMAGINE someday working at a cyber security company, fire station, police department, or prison?

ARE YOU CURIOUS ABOUT what animal control officers, coroners, detectives, firefighters, or park rangers do?

Manufacturing

WOULD YOU ENJOY figuring out how things are made, competing in a robot-building contest, or putting model airplanes together?

CAN YOU IMAGINE someday working at a high-tech manufacturing plant, engineering firm, or global logistics company?

ARE YOU CURIOUS ABOUT what chemical engineers, industrial designers, supply chain managers, robotics technologists, or welders do?

Marketing, Sales & Service

WOULD YOU ENJOY keeping up with the latest fashion trends, picking favorite TV commercials during Super Bowl games, or making posters for a favorite school club?

CAN YOU IMAGINE someday working at an advertising agency, corporate marketing department, or retail store?

ARE YOU CURIOUS ABOUT what creative directors, market researchers, media buyers, retail store managers, and social media consultants do?

Science, Technology, Engineering & Mathematics (STEM)

WOULD YOU ENJOY concocting experiments in a science lab, trying out the latest smartphone, or taking advanced math classes?

CAN YOU IMAGINE someday working in a science laboratory, engineering firm, or research and development center?

ARE YOU CURIOUS ABOUT what aeronautical engineers, ecologists, statisticians, oceanographers, or zoologists do?

Transportation

WOULD YOU ENJOY taking pilot or sailing lessons, watching a NASA rocket launch, or helping out in the school carpool lane?

CAN YOU IMAGINE someday working at an airport, mass transit system, or shipping port?

ARE YOU CURIOUS ABOUT what air traffic controllers, flight attendants, logistics planners, surveyors, and traffic engineers do?

MY WoW

I am here.

Name _____

Grade _____

School _____

Who I am.

Make a word collage! Use 5 adjectives to form a picture that describes who you are.

Where I'm going.

The next career pathway I want to explore is

_____

Some things I need to learn first to succeed.

1 _____

2 _____

3 _____

My Career Choice

To get here.

GLOSSARY

administration
the activity of managing all the details of something, such as a business or project

after-school care
program that takes place for children immediately after the school day is over

animal trainer
person who teaches animals to do something, be capable of something, or behave in a certain way

Caldecott
an award given to an artist who creates an outstanding American picture book for children

child care director
person who manages a child care center

coach
person who trains someone in a sport, skill, or subject

distance learning coordinator
person who manages online educational programs

elementary teacher
person who instructs children in kindergarten through fifth grades

foundation
solid structure on which something can be built

media specialist
person who runs a school library that has technology along with written materials

Newbery
an award given to authors of books that make an important contribution to American literature for children

payroll
a list of workers who are paid by a company, along with the amount each is to be paid

peer mediation
the process of students helping other students solve problems

principal
person who is the head of a school

school counselor
person who works in elementary, middle, or high schools to provide academic, career, and college readiness help, as well as help with personal and social issues

therapy
a treatment for an illness, injury, disability, or psychological problem

INDEX

*Animal Planet, 9

Architecture & Construction, 5, 27

Arts & Communication, 5, 27

*Berra, Yogi, 13

*Bio, 19

Business Administration, 5, 27

*Caldecott Award, 19

*Carnegie Foundation, 21

*Dr Math, 17

*Dr Seuss, 19

*e-Learning for Kids, 15

Finance, 5, 27

*First Gov for Kids, 17

Food & Natural Resources, 5, 27

*Francis Howell School District, 21

*Granite Schools, 15

Health Science, 5, 28

Hospitality & Tourism 5, 28

Human Resources, 5, 28

Information Technology, 5, 28

*Kryzewski, Mike, 13

Landry, Tom, 13

Law & Public Safety, 5, 29

Lombardi, Vince, 13

Manufacturing, 5, 29

*Math Forum, 17

*My Next Move, 23

*National Geographic, 9, 17

*Newbery Award, 19

*Pacer Kids Against Bullying, 23

*PBS It's My Life, 23

*Red Cross, 11

*Rowling, JK, 19

Science, Technology, Engineering & Mathematics, 5, 29

*Stine, RL, 19

Transportation, 5, 29

*U.S. Department of Labor, 23

*Wallace Foundation, 21

*Wooden, John, 13

*YMCA, 11

*Zoo Online, The, 9

* Refers to the Web page sources

About the Author

Diane Lindsey Reeves is the author of lots of children's books. She has written several original PEANUTS stories (published by Regnery Kids and Sourcebooks). She is especially curious about what people do and likes to write books that get kids thinking about all the cool things they can be when they grow up. She lives in Cary, North Carolina, and her favorite thing to do is play with her grandkids—Conrad, Evan, Reid, and Hollis Grace.